This journal belongs to: _____

Address: _____

Phone: _____

Email: _____

Tackle Checklist

- ◯ Fishing license
- ◯ Bag
- ◯ Rod and reel (extra)
- ◯ Lures
- ◯ Hooks
- ◯ Jigs
- ◯ Bait
- ◯ Line
- ◯ Fishing net
- ◯ Pliers
- ◯ Knife
- ◯ Stringers

- ◯ Fish Finder

- ◯ Super glue gel

- ◯ Rod tip extras

- ◯ Sunglasses
- ◯ Hat
- ◯ Rain gear
- ◯ Footgear
- ◯ Gloves

- ◯ First aid kit
- ◯ Duct tape
- ◯ Phone
- ◯ Flashlight

- ◯ Sunscreen
- ◯ Insect repellent
- ◯ Lip balm

- ◯ Towel
- ◯ Hand sanitizer
- ◯ Toilet paper or wipes

An Angler's Journal

How to Use This Journal

The main feature is the Expedition Log. Each new entry in the expedition log is two pages. The left-side page suggests key facts to record about your expedition, and has room for extra notes. On the right-side page, there is a blank space for you to either draw or paste a picture of each fishing location. This way, at the end of the day, you can mark out "honey holes" and record the depths where fish were found, along with other data. You can create this picture before, during, or after your fishing expedition—whichever works best for you. Here are several ideas for creating pictures of your fishing locations:

 • Print out a Google maps satellite photo, labels off, sized to fit the 6" x 8" page. Pen or marker will work best for annotating.

 • Sketch the location by hand using graphite sketch pencils. You may want to add color, or add stronger lines by using pens or markers.

 • Copy or cut out part of a physical map and either tape or glue it to your page. Pen or marker will work best for annotating.

 • Snap a photo with your camera or phone and order a print, then paste or tape it to the page. You can use margin space to write in labels.

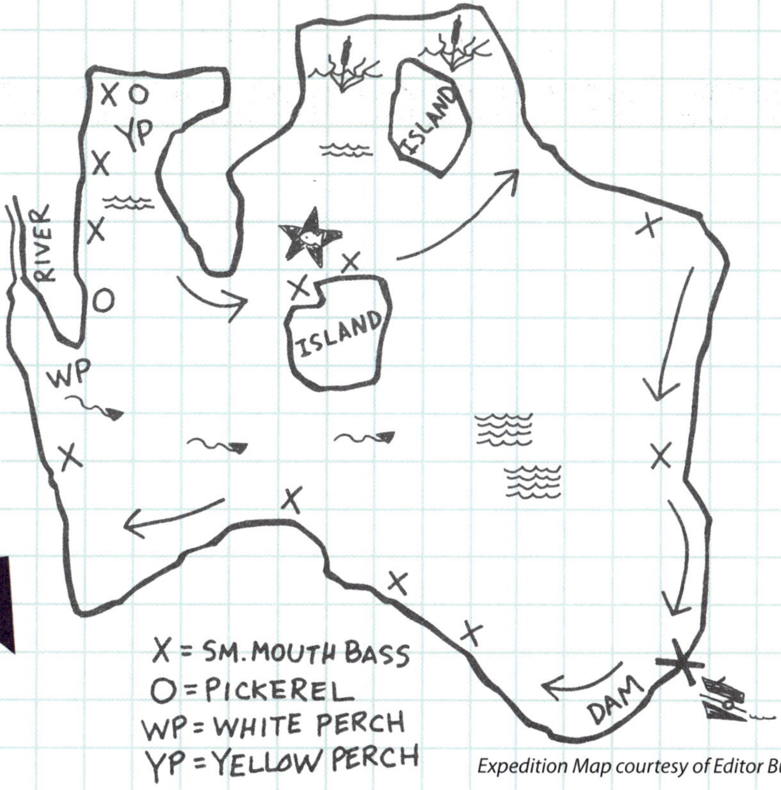

X O
YP

X

RIVER

X

O

WP

X

ISLAND

ISLAND

X

X

X

X

X

X

X

X

X

X

DAM

X = SM. MOUTH BASS
O = PICKEREL
WP = WHITE PERCH
YP = YELLOW PERCH

Expedition Map courtesy of Editor Bud Sperry

As you progress along your angling journey, you may enjoy using the lists in the back of the journal to track important events. For example, use the Fishing Life List (pages 122-139) to keep a record of which species you have caught, and which ones you have yet to catch. You will then be able to cross-reference the list by date to the specific expedition where you caught each kind of fish. You may find that keeping a record of changes in and successes with your fishing equipment will help improve your angling abilities. Finally, have fun adding photos of your greatest catches to the Gallery section, using tape or glue. By using this journal, you will become a more attentive angler, and you will enjoy your angling memories for years to come.

Happy fishing!

Legend:

Deep Water

Shallow Water

Current Flow

Boat Launch

Weeds

Honey Hole

Rods & Reels

Brand	Date of Purchase	Description

Brand	Date of Purchase	Description

Lures & Bait

Lure/Bait	Weight	Date of Purchase	Target Fish

Lure/Bait	Weight	Date of Purchase	Target Fish

Knot-Tying Basics

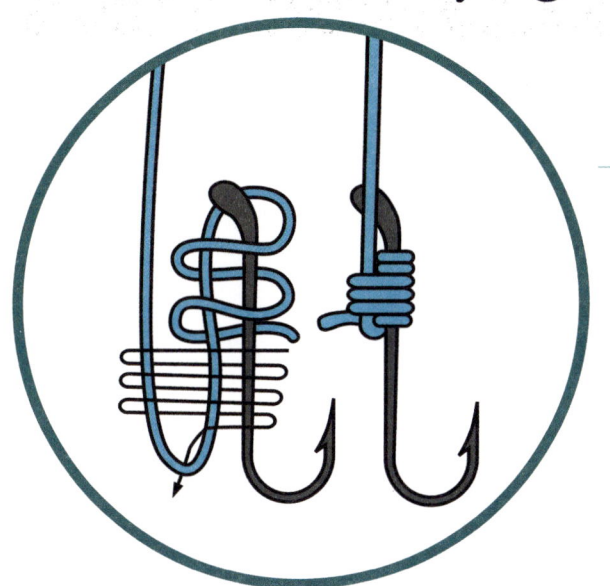

Snell Knot

Use this clean, simple knot especially when your hook doesn't have an eye with a hole in it, or when you're using tandem hooks.

Clinch Knot

One of the most common knots in fishing and good for fly-fishing as well as angling; a knot every angler should know.

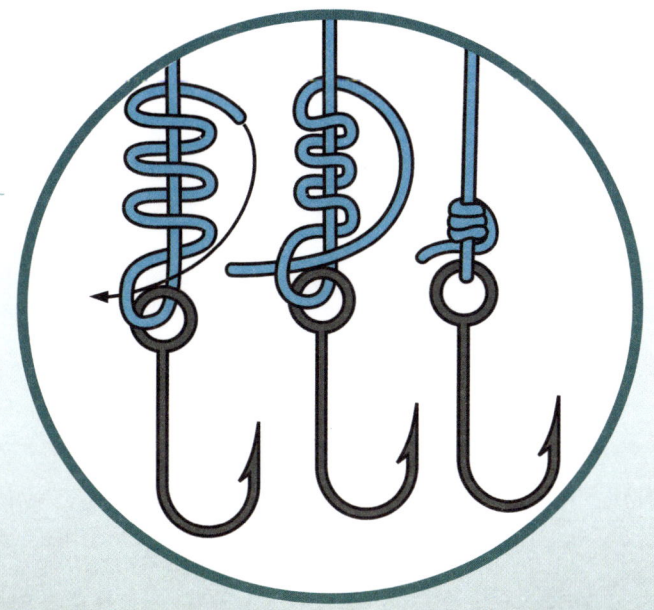

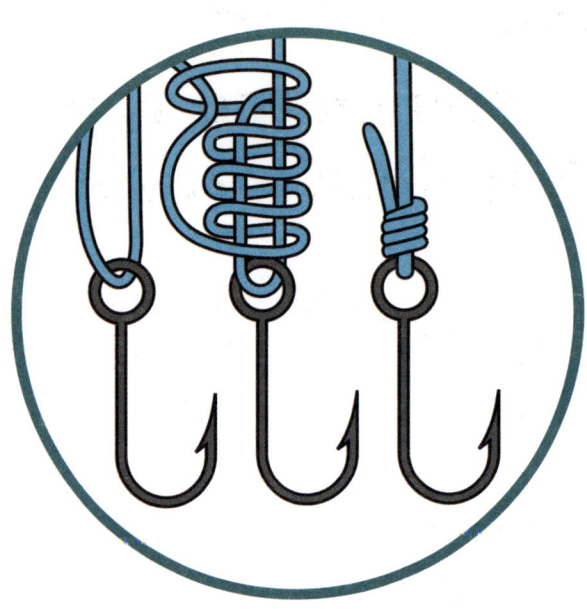

Hangman's Knot

Also called the Uni Knot, excellent and simple for attaching monofilament line to tackle.

Turle Knot

Named after famed English angler Major William Greer Turle; excellent for tying flies to line.

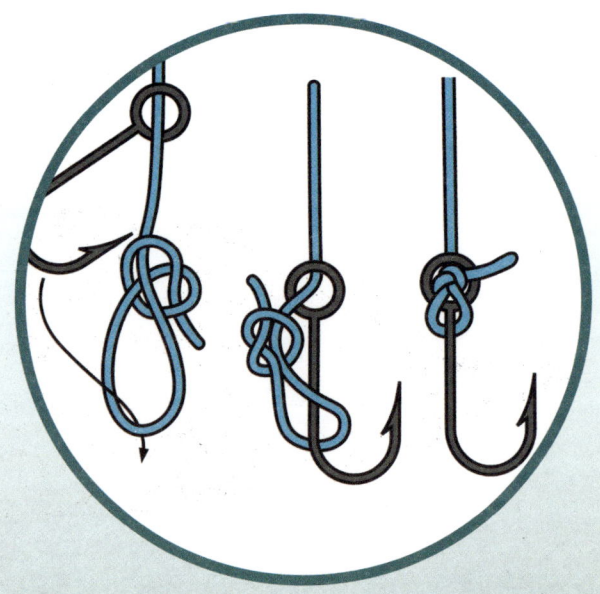

Expedition Log
Log your expeditions so you can remember them forever

False Albacore

Northern Pike

California Yellowtail

Beaver Pond Brook Trout

Date: _____ Start: _____ Finish: _____ Temperature: _____

Weather: _____ GPS coordinates: _____

Location: _____

Fishing with: _____

Target fish: _____

Fish Caught	Length	Weight	Lure & Bait

Notes: _____
_____
_____
_____

Legend:

≈≈≈ Deep Water ≈ Shallow Water ∿→ Current Flow 🛥 Boat Launch 🌿 Weeds ★ Honey Hole

Date: _____ Start: _____ Finish: _____ Temperature: _____

Weather: _____ GPS coordinates: _____

Location: _____

Fishing with: _____

Target fish: _____

Fish Caught	Length	Weight	Lure & Bait

Notes: _____

_____

_____

_____

Deep Water   Shallow Water   Current Flow   Boat Launch   Weeds   Honey Hole

Date: _____ Start: _____ Finish: _____ Temperature: _____

Weather: _____ GPS coordinates: _____

Location: _____

Fishing with: _____

Target fish: _____

Fish Caught	Length	Weight	Lure & Bait

Notes: _____

_____

_____

_____

Legend:

Deep Water   Shallow Water   Current Flow   Boat Launch   Weeds   Honey Hole

Date: _____ Start: _____ Finish: _____ Temperature: _____

Weather: _____ GPS coordinates: _____

Location: _____

Fishing with: _____

Target fish: _____

Fish Caught	Length	Weight	Lure & Bait

Notes: _____

_____

_____

_____

_____

Legend:

Deep Water   Shallow Water   Current Flow   Boat Launch   Weeds   Honey Hole

Date: _____ Start: _____ Finish: _____ Temperature: _____

Weather: _____ GPS coordinates: _____

Location: _____

Fishing with: _____

Target fish: _____

Fish Caught	Length	Weight	Lure & Bait

Notes: _____

_____

_____

_____

_____

Date: _____ Start: _____ Finish: _____ Temperature: _____

Weather: _____ GPS coordinates: _____

Location: _____

Fishing with: _____

Target fish: _____

Fish Caught	Length	Weight	Lure & Bait

Notes: _____
_____
_____
_____
_____

Legend:

Deep Water   Shallow Water   Current Flow   Boat Launch   Weeds   Honey Hole

Date: _____ Start: _____ Finish: _____ Temperature: _____

Weather: _____ GPS coordinates: _____

Location: _____

Fishing with: _____

Target fish: _____

Fish Caught	Length	Weight	Lure & Bait

Notes: _____
_____
_____
_____
_____

Legend:

Deep Water   Shallow Water   Current Flow   Boat Launch   Weeds   Honey Hole

Date: _____ Start: _____ Finish: _____ Temperature: _____

Weather: _____ GPS coordinates: _____

Location: _____

Fishing with: _____

Target fish: _____

Fish Caught	Length	Weight	Lure & Bait

Notes: _____
_____
_____
_____
_____

Legend:

〰〰〰 Deep Water   〰 Shallow Water   ∿➤ Current Flow   ⛵ Boat Launch   🪻 Weeds   ★ Honey Hole

Date: _____ Start: _____ Finish: _____ Temperature: _____

Weather: _____ GPS coordinates: _____

Location: _____

Fishing with: _____

Target fish: _____

Fish Caught	Length	Weight	Lure & Bait

Notes: _____
_____
_____
_____
_____

Legend:

Deep Water   Shallow Water   Current Flow   Boat Launch   Weeds   Honey Hole

Date: _____ Start: _____ Finish: _____ Temperature: _____

Weather: _____ GPS coordinates: _____

Location: _____

Fishing with: _____

Target fish: _____

Fish Caught	Length	Weight	Lure & Bait

Notes: _____

_____

_____

_____

_____

Legend:

Deep Water Shallow Water Current Flow Boat Launch Weeds Honey Hole

Date: _____ Start: _____ Finish: _____ Temperature: _____

Weather: _____ GPS coordinates: _____

Location: _____

Fishing with: _____

Target fish: _____

Fish Caught	Length	Weight	Lure & Bait

Notes: _____
_____
_____
_____
_____

Legend:

Deep Water   Shallow Water   Current Flow   Boat Launch   Weeds   Honey Hole

Date: _____ Start: _____ Finish: _____ Temperature: _____

Weather: _____ GPS coordinates: _____

Location: _____

Fishing with: _____

Target fish: _____

Fish Caught	Length	Weight	Lure & Bait

Notes: _____

_____

_____

_____

_____

Legend:

Deep Water   Shallow Water   Current Flow   Boat Launch   Weeds   Honey Hole

Date: _____ Start: _____ Finish: _____ Temperature: _____

Weather: _____ GPS coordinates: _____

Location: _____

Fishing with: _____

Target fish: _____

Fish Caught	Length	Weight	Lure & Bait

Notes: _____
_____
_____
_____

Legend:

Deep Water   Shallow Water   Current Flow   Boat Launch   Weeds   Honey Hole

Date: _____ Start: _____ Finish: _____ Temperature: _____

Weather: _____ GPS coordinates: _____

Location: _____

Fishing with: _____

Target fish: _____

Fish Caught	Length	Weight	Lure & Bait

Notes: _____
_____
_____
_____
_____

Legend:

Deep Water   Shallow Water   Current Flow   Boat Launch   Weeds   Honey Hole

Date: _____ Start: _____ Finish: _____ Temperature: _____

Weather: _____ GPS coordinates: _____

Location: _____

Fishing with: _____

Target fish: _____

Fish Caught	Length	Weight	Lure & Bait

Notes: _____

_____

_____

_____

Legend:

Deep Water   Shallow Water   Current Flow   Boat Launch   Weeds   Honey Hole

Date: _____ Start: _____ Finish: _____ Temperature: _____

Weather: _____ GPS coordinates: _____

Location: _____

Fishing with: _____

Target fish: _____

Fish Caught	Length	Weight	Lure & Bait

Notes: _____
_____
_____
_____
_____

Legend:

Deep Water   Shallow Water   Current Flow   Boat Launch   Weeds   Honey Hole

Date: _____ Start: _____ Finish: _____ Temperature: _____

Weather: _____ GPS coordinates: _____

Location: _____

Fishing with: _____

Target fish: _____

Fish Caught	Length	Weight	Lure & Bait

Notes: _____
_____
_____
_____
_____

Legend:

〜〜〜 Deep Water

〜〜 Shallow Water

〜〜➤ Current Flow

🚤 Boat Launch

🌿 Weeds

⭐ Honey Hole

Date: _____ Start: _____ Finish: _____ Temperature: _____

Weather: _____ GPS coordinates: _____

Location: _____

Fishing with: _____

Target fish: _____

Fish Caught	Length	Weight	Lure & Bait

Notes: _____

_____

_____

_____

_____

Legend:

Deep Water　　Shallow Water　　Current Flow　　Boat Launch　　Weeds　　Honey Hole

Date: _____ Start: _____ Finish: _____ Temperature: _____

Weather: _____ GPS coordinates: _____

Location: _____

Fishing with: _____

Target fish: _____

Fish Caught	Length	Weight	Lure & Bait

Notes: _____
_____
_____
_____
_____

Date: _____ Start: _____ Finish: _____ Temperature: _____

Weather: _____ GPS coordinates: _____

Location: _____

Fishing with: _____

Target fish: _____

Fish Caught	Length	Weight	Lure & Bait

Notes: _____
_____
_____
_____
_____

Legend:

Deep Water   Shallow Water   Current Flow   Boat Launch   Weeds   Honey Hole

Date: _____ Start: _____ Finish: _____ Temperature: _____

Weather: _____ GPS coordinates: _____

Location: _____

Fishing with: _____

Target fish: _____

Fish Caught	Length	Weight	Lure & Bait

Notes: _____

_____

_____

_____

_____

Legend:

Deep Water Shallow Water Current Flow Boat Launch Weeds Honey Hole

Date: _____ Start: _____ Finish: _____ Temperature: _____

Weather: _____ GPS coordinates: _____

Location: _____

Fishing with: _____

Target fish: _____

Fish Caught	Length	Weight	Lure & Bait

Notes: _____
_____
_____
_____
_____

Legend:

≈≈≈ Deep Water   ∼∼∼ Shallow Water   ∼∼↗ Current Flow   🛥 Boat Launch   🌿 Weeds   ★ Honey Hole

Date: _____ Start: _____ Finish: _____ Temperature: _____

Weather: _____ GPS coordinates: _____

Location: _____

Fishing with: _____

Target fish: _____

Fish Caught	Length	Weight	Lure & Bait

Notes: _____
_____
_____
_____
_____

Legend:

Deep Water   Shallow Water   Current Flow   Boat Launch   Weeds   Honey Hole

Date: _____ Start: _____ Finish: _____ Temperature: _____

Weather: _____ GPS coordinates: _____

Location: _____

Fishing with: _____

Target fish: _____

Fish Caught	Length	Weight	Lure & Bait

Notes: _____
_____
_____
_____
_____

Legend:

Deep Water Shallow Water Current Flow Boat Launch Weeds Honey Hole

Date: _____ Start: _____ Finish: _____ Temperature: _____

Weather: _____ GPS coordinates: _____

Location: _____

Fishing with: _____

Target fish: _____

Fish Caught	Length	Weight	Lure & Bait

Notes: _____

_____

_____

_____

Legend:

Deep Water Shallow Water Current Flow Boat Launch Weeds Honey Hole

Date: _____ Start: _____ Finish: _____ Temperature: _____

Weather: _____ GPS coordinates: _____

Location: _____

Fishing with: _____

Target fish: _____

Fish Caught	Length	Weight	Lure & Bait

Notes: _____

_____

_____

_____

_____

Legend:

Deep Water   Shallow Water   Current Flow   Boat Launch   Weeds   Honey Hole

Date: _____ Start: _____ Finish: _____ Temperature: _____

Weather: _____ GPS coordinates: _____

Location: _____

Fishing with: _____

Target fish: _____

Fish Caught	Length	Weight	Lure & Bait

Notes: _____

_____

_____

_____

_____

Legend:

Deep Water   Shallow Water   Current Flow   Boat Launch   Weeds   Honey Hole

Date:_____ Start:_____ Finish:_____ Temperature:_____

Weather:_____ GPS coordinates:_____

Location:_____

Fishing with:_____

Target fish:_____

Fish Caught	Length	Weight	Lure & Bait

Notes:_____

_____

_____

_____

_____

Legend:

Deep Water Shallow Water Current Flow Boat Launch Weeds Honey Hole

Date: _____ Start: _____ Finish: _____ Temperature: _____

Weather: _____ GPS coordinates: _____

Location: _____

Fishing with: _____

Target fish: _____

Fish Caught	Length	Weight	Lure & Bait

Notes: _____
_____
_____
_____
_____

Legend:

Deep Water   Shallow Water   Current Flow   Boat Launch   Weeds   Honey Hole

Date: _____ Start: _____ Finish: _____ Temperature: _____

Weather: _____ GPS coordinates: _____

Location: _____

Fishing with: _____

Target fish: _____

Fish Caught	Length	Weight	Lure & Bait

Notes: _____

_____

_____

_____

Legend:

Deep Water Shallow Water Current Flow Boat Launch Weeds Honey Hole

Date: _____ Start: _____ Finish: _____ Temperature: _____

Weather: _____ GPS coordinates: _____

Location: _____

Fishing with: _____

Target fish: _____

Fish Caught	Length	Weight	Lure & Bait

Notes: _____
_____
_____
_____
_____

Date: _____ Start: _____ Finish: _____ Temperature: _____

Weather: _____ GPS coordinates: _____

Location: _____

Fishing with: _____

Target fish: _____

Fish Caught	Length	Weight	Lure & Bait

Notes: _____
_____
_____
_____
_____

Legend:

Deep Water   Shallow Water   Current Flow   Boat Launch   Weeds   Honey Hole

Date: _____ Start: _____ Finish: _____ Temperature: _____

Weather: _____ GPS coordinates: _____

Location: _____

Fishing with: _____

Target fish: _____

Fish Caught	Length	Weight	Lure & Bait

Notes: _____
_____
_____
_____
_____

Legend:

Deep Water   Shallow Water   Current Flow   Boat Launch   Weeds   Honey Hole

Date: _____ Start: _____ Finish: _____ Temperature: _____

Weather: _____ GPS coordinates: _____

Location: _____

Fishing with: _____

Target fish: _____

Fish Caught	Length	Weight	Lure & Bait

Notes: _____

_____

_____

_____

_____

Legend:

Deep Water   Shallow Water   Current Flow   Boat Launch   Weeds   Honey Hole

Date: _____ Start: _____ Finish: _____ Temperature: _____

Weather: _____ GPS coordinates: _____

Location: _____

Fishing with: _____

Target fish: _____

Fish Caught	Length	Weight	Lure & Bait

Notes: _____
_____
_____
_____
_____

Legend:

Deep Water Shallow Water Current Flow Boat Launch Weeds Honey Hole

Date: _____ Start: _____ Finish: _____ Temperature: _____

Weather: _____ GPS coordinates: _____

Location: _____

Fishing with: _____

Target fish: _____

Fish Caught	Length	Weight	Lure & Bait

Notes: _____
_____
_____
_____
_____

Legend:

Deep Water   Shallow Water   Current Flow   Boat Launch   Weeds   Honey Hole

Date: _____ Start: _____ Finish: _____ Temperature: _____

Weather: _____ GPS coordinates: _____

Location: _____

Fishing with: _____

Target fish: _____

Fish Caught	Length	Weight	Lure & Bait

Notes: _____
_____
_____
_____
_____

Legend:

Deep Water | Shallow Water | Current Flow | Boat Launch | Weeds | Honey Hole

Date: _____ Start: _____ Finish: _____ Temperature: _____

Weather: _____ GPS coordinates: _____

Location: _____

Fishing with: _____

Target fish: _____

Fish Caught	Length	Weight	Lure & Bait

Notes: _____

_____

_____

_____

_____

Legend:

Deep Water	Shallow Water	Current Flow	Boat Launch	Weeds	Honey Hole

Date: _____ Start: _____ Finish: _____ Temperature: _____

Weather: _____ GPS coordinates: _____

Location: _____

Fishing with: _____

Target fish: _____

Fish Caught	Length	Weight	Lure & Bait

Notes: _____
_____
_____
_____
_____

Legend:

Deep Water Shallow Water Current Flow Boat Launch Weeds Honey Hole

Date: _____ Start: _____ Finish: _____ Temperature: _____

Weather: _____ GPS coordinates: _____

Location: _____

Fishing with: _____

Target fish: _____

Fish Caught	Length	Weight	Lure & Bait

Notes: _____
_____
_____
_____
_____

Legend:

Deep Water   Shallow Water   Current Flow   Boat Launch   Weeds   Honey Hole

Date: _____ Start: _____ Finish: _____ Temperature: _____

Weather: _____ GPS coordinates: _____

Location: _____

Fishing with: _____

Target fish: _____

Fish Caught	Length	Weight	Lure & Bait

Notes: _____
_____
_____
_____

Legend:

Deep Water   Shallow Water   Current Flow   Boat Launch   Weeds   Honey Hole

Date: _____ Start: _____ Finish: _____ Temperature: _____

Weather: _____ GPS coordinates: _____

Location: _____

Fishing with: _____

Target fish: _____

Fish Caught	Length	Weight	Lure & Bait

Notes: _____

_____

_____

_____

_____

Legend:

Deep Water   Shallow Water   Current Flow   Boat Launch   Weeds   Honey Hole

Date: _____ Start: _____ Finish: _____ Temperature: _____

Weather: _____ GPS coordinates: _____

Location: _____

Fishing with: _____

Target fish: _____

Fish Caught	Length	Weight	Lure & Bait

Notes: _____

_____

_____

_____

_____

Date: _____ Start: _____ Finish: _____ Temperature: _____

Weather: _____ GPS coordinates: _____

Location: _____

Fishing with: _____

Target fish: _____

Fish Caught	Length	Weight	Lure & Bait

Notes: _____

_____

_____

_____

_____

Legend:

Deep Water   Shallow Water   Current Flow   Boat Launch   Weeds   Honey Hole

Date: _____ Start: _____ Finish: _____ Temperature: _____

Weather: _____ GPS coordinates: _____

Location: _____

Fishing with: _____

Target fish: _____

Fish Caught	Length	Weight	Lure & Bait

Notes: _____

_____

_____

_____

_____

Legend:

Deep Water   Shallow Water   Current Flow   Boat Launch   Weeds   Honey Hole

Date: _____ Start: _____ Finish: _____ Temperature: _____

Weather: _____ GPS coordinates: _____

Location: _____

Fishing with: _____

Target fish: _____

Fish Caught	Length	Weight	Lure & Bait

Notes: _____

_____

_____

_____

_____

Legend:

Deep Water   Shallow Water   Current Flow   Boat Launch   Weeds   Honey Hole

Date: _____ Start: _____ Finish: _____ Temperature: _____

Weather: _____ GPS coordinates: _____

Location: _____

Fishing with: _____

Target fish: _____

Fish Caught	Length	Weight	Lure & Bait

Notes: _____

_____

_____

_____

_____

Legend:

Deep Water　　Shallow Water　　Current Flow　　Boat Launch　　Weeds　　Honey Hole

Date: _____ Start: _____ Finish: _____ Temperature: _____

Weather: _____ GPS coordinates: _____

Location: _____

Fishing with: _____

Target fish: _____

Fish Caught	Length	Weight	Lure & Bait

Notes: _____

_____

_____

_____

_____

Legend:

Deep Water   Shallow Water   Current Flow   Boat Launch   Weeds   Honey Hole

Date: _____ Start: _____ Finish: _____ Temperature: _____

Weather: _____ GPS coordinates: _____

Location: _____

Fishing with: _____

Target fish: _____

Fish Caught	Length	Weight	Lure & Bait

Notes: _____

_____

_____

_____

_____

Legend:

Deep Water — Shallow Water — Current Flow — Boat Launch — Weeds — Honey Hole

Date: _____ Start: _____ Finish: _____ Temperature: _____

Weather: _____ GPS coordinates: _____

Location: _____

Fishing with: _____

Target fish: _____

Fish Caught	Length	Weight	Lure & Bait

Notes: _____

_____

_____

_____

_____

Legend:

≋ Deep Water   ∿ Shallow Water   ∿→ Current Flow   🚤 Boat Launch   🌿 Weeds   ⭐ Honey Hole

Date: _____ Start: _____ Finish: _____ Temperature: _____

Weather: _____ GPS coordinates: _____

Location: _____

Fishing with: _____

Target fish: _____

Fish Caught	Length	Weight	Lure & Bait

Notes: _____
_____
_____
_____
_____

Legend:

≋ Deep Water   ∿ Shallow Water   ➤ Current Flow   ⛴ Boat Launch   🌿 Weeds   ⭐ Honey Hole

Date: _____ Time out: _____ Time in: _____ Temperature: _____

Weather: _____ GPS Coordinates: _____

Location: _____

Fishing with: _____

Target Fish: _____

Fish Caught	Length	Weight	Lure & Bait

Notes: _____

_____

_____

_____

_____

Legend:

Deep Water Shallow Water Current Flow Boat Launch Weeds Honey Hole

Date: _____ Time out: _____ Time in: _____ Temperature: _____

Weather: _____ GPS Coordinates: _____

Location: _____

Fishing with: _____

Target Fish: _____

Fish Caught	Length	Weight	Lure & Bait

Notes: _____
_____
_____
_____
_____

Legend:

Deep Water   Shallow Water   Current Flow   Boat Launch   Weeds   Honey Hole

Date: _____ Time out: _____ Time in: _____ Temperature: _____

Weather: _____ GPS Coordinates: _____

Location: _____

Fishing with: _____

Target Fish: _____

Fish Caught	Length	Weight	Lure & Bait

Notes: _____

_____

_____

_____

_____

Legend:

Deep Water   Shallow Water   Current Flow   Boat Launch   Weeds   Honey Hole

Date: _____ Time out: _____ Time in: _____ Temperature: _____

Weather: _____ GPS Coordinates: _____

Location: _____

Fishing with: _____

Target Fish: _____

Fish Caught	Length	Weight	Lure & Bait

Notes: _____

_____

_____

_____

Legend:

Deep Water   Shallow Water   Current Flow   Boat Launch   Weeds   Honey Hole

Date: _____ Time out: _____ Time in: _____ Temperature: _____

Weather: _____ GPS Coordinates: _____

Location: _____

Fishing with: _____

Target Fish: _____

Fish Caught	Length	Weight	Lure & Bait

Notes: _____

_____

_____

_____

Legend:

Deep Water   Shallow Water   Current Flow   Boat Launch   Weeds   Honey Hole

Fishing Life List

Keep track of which species you have caught—and which ones are still out there!

Largemouth
Bass

Yellowfin Tuna

Mackerel

Tarpon

Fishing Life List

Species	Date	Lure/Bait	Specs	Location
Albacore *(Thunnus alalunga)*				
Amazon Pellona *(Pellona castelnaeana)*				
Amberjack, Greater *(Seriola dumerili)*				
Arawana *(Osteoglossum bicirrhosum)*				
Artic grayling *(Thymallus arcticus)*				
Asp *(Aspius aspius)*				
Atlantic Spadefish *(Chaetodipterus faber)*				
Barbel *(Barbus barbus)*				
Barracuda				
Great *(Sphyraena barracuda)*				
Guinean *(Sphyraena afra)*				
Mexican *(Sphyraena ensis)*				
Barramundi *(Lates calcarifer)*				
Bass				
Australian *(Percalates novemaculeata)*				
Black Sea *(Centropristis striata)*				
European *(Dicentrarchus labrax)*				
Giant Sea *(Stereolepis gigas)*				
Kelp *(Paralabrax clathratus)*				
Largemouth *(Micropterus salmoides)*				
Rock *(Ambloplites rupestris)*				
Shoal *(Micropterus cataractae)*				
Smallmouth *(Micropterus dolomieu)*				
Spotted *(Micropterus punctulatus)*				
Striped *(Morone saxatilis)*				
White *(Morone chrysops)*				
Whiterock *(Morone saxatilis x M. chrysops)*				
Yellow *(Morone mississippiensis)*				
Bluefish *(Pomatomus saltatrix)*				
Bluegill *(Lepomis macrochirus)*				
Bonefish *(Albula vulpes)*				
Bonito				
Atlantic *(Sarda sarda)*				
Pacific *(Sarda lineolata)*				
Bowfin *(Amia calva)*				

Species	Date	Lure/Bait	Specs	Location
Buffalo				
Bigmouth (Ictiobus cyprinellus)				
Smallmouth (Ictiobus bubalus)				
Bullhead				
Black (Ameiurus melas)				
Brown (Ameiurus nebulosus)				
Yellow (Ameiurus natalis)				
Burbot (Lota lota)				
Buri (Seriola quinqueradiata)				
Carp				
Common (Cyprinus carpio)				
Grass (Ctenopharyngodo idella)				
Black (Mylopharyngodon piceus)				
Catfish				
Channel (Ictalurus punctatus)				
Flathead (Ameiurus melas)				
Redtail (Pylodictis olivaris)				
Sharptooth (Clarias gariepinus)				
White (Ameiurus catus)				
California Yellowtail (Seriola lalandi)				
Chain Pickerel (Esox niger)				
Char, Arctic (Salvelinus alpinus)				
Cobia (Rachyncentron canadum)				
Cod				
Atlantic (Gadus morhua)				
Pacific (Gadus macrocephalus)				
Conger, American (Conger oceanicus)				
Corbina, California (Menticirrhus undulatus)				
Crappie				
Black (Pomoxis nigromaculatus)				
White (Pomoxis annularis)				
Dentex Dentex dentex				
Drum				
Black (Pogonias cromis)				
Freshwater (Aplodinotus grunniens)				

Fishing Life List

Species	Date	Lure/Bait	Specs	Location
Red (Sciaenops ocellatus)				
Flounder				
Cresthead (Pseudopleuronectes schrenki)				
Summer (Paralichthys dentatus)				
Gar				
Alligator (Atractosteus spatula)				
Florida (Lepisosteus platyrhincus)				
Longnose (Lepisosteus osseus)				
Shortnose (Lepisosteus platostomus)				
Spotted (Lepisosteus oculatus)				
Grouper				
Black (Mycteroperca bonaci)				
Broomtail (Mycteroperca xenarcha)				
Gag (Mycteroperca microlepis)				
Goliath (Epinephelus itajara)				
Red (Epinephelus morio)				
Gilt-Head Seabream (Sparus aurata)				
Halibut				
Atlantic (Hippoglossus hippoglossus)				
California (Paralichthys californicus)				
Huchen (Hucho hucho)				
Inconnu (Stenodus leucichthys)				
Jack				
Almaco (Seriola rivoliana)				
Crevalle (Caranx hippos)				
Horse-eye (Caranx latus)				
Pacific Crevalle (Caranx caninus)				
Japanese Parrotperch (Oplegnathus fasciatus)				
Kahawai (Arripis trutta)				
Leerfish (Lichia amia)				
Lingcod (Ophiodon elongatus)				
Little Tunny (Euthynnus alletteratus)				
Mackerel				
Atlantic Spanish (Scomberomorus maculatus)				
Cero (Scomberomorus regalis)				

Species	Date	Lure/Bait	Specs	Location
King (Scomberomorus cavalla)				
Narrow-barred (Scomberomorus commerson)				
Pacific Sierra (Scomberomorus sierra)				
Mackerel Tuna (Euthynnus affinis)				
Madai Snapper (Pagrus major)				
Mahi-mahi (Coryphaena hippurus)				
Marlin				
Black (Istiompax indica)				
Atlantic Blue (Makaira nigricans)				
Indo-Pacific Blue (Makaira mazara)				
Striped (Kajikia audax)				
White (Kajikia albidus)				
Meagre (Argyrosomus regius)				
Muskellunge (Esox masquinongy)				
Nembwe (Serranochromis robustus)				
Northern Pike (Esox lucius)				
Oscar (Astronotus ocellatus)				
Pacific Ladyfish (Elops affinis)				
Payara (Hydrolycus scomberoides)				
Peacock Bass				
Blackstriped (Cichla intermedia)				
Butterfly (Cichla ocellaris)				
Orinoco (Cichla orinocensis)				
Speckled (Cichla temensis)				
Perch				
European (Perca fluviatilis)				
Nile (Lates niloticus)				
White (Morone americana)				
Yellow (Perca flavescens)				
Permit (Trachinotus falcatus)				
Pollock (Pollachius pollachius)				
Pompano				
African (Alectis ciliaris)				
Florida (Trachinotus carolinus)				
Queenfish				

Fishing Life List

Species	Date	Lure/Bait	Specs	Location
Doublespotted (Scomberoides lysan)				
Talang (Scomberoides commersonnianus)				
Rainbow Runner (Elagatis bipinnulata)				
Red-Bellied Piranha (Pygocentrus nattereri)				
Redhorse				
Shorthead (Moxostoma macrolepidotum)				
Silver (Moxostoma anisurum)				
Rockfish				
Blue (Sebastes mystinus)				
Yelloweye (Sebastes ruberrimus)				
Roosterfish (Nematistius pectoralis)				
Sailfish				
Atlantic (Istiophorus albicans)				
Indo-Pacific (Istiophorus platypterus)				
Salmon				
Landlocked Atlantic (Salmo salar)				
Chinook (Oncorhynchus tshawytscha)				
Chum (Oncorhynchus keta)				
Coho (Oncorhynchus kisutch)				
Pink (Oncorhynchus gorbuscha)				
Sockeye (Oncorhynchus nerka)				
Samson Fish (Seriola hippos)				
Sauger (Sander Canadensis)				
Seabass				
Blackfin (Lateolabrax latus)				
Japanese (Lateolabrax japonicas)				
White (Atractoscion nobilis)				
Shad				
American (Alosa sapidissima)				
Hickory (Alosa mediocris)				
Snakehead (Channidae spp.)				
Snapper				
African Red (Lutjanus agennes)				
Cubera (Lutjanus cyanopterus)				
Gray (Lutjanus griseus)				

Species	Date	Lure/Bait	Specs	Location
Mullet (Lutjanus analis)				
Pacific Cubera (Lutjanus novemfasciatus)				
Papuan Black (Lutjanus goldiei)				
Red (Lutjanus campechanus)				
Yellowtail (Ocyurus chrysurus)				
Snook				
Common (Centropomus undecimalis)				
Pacific (Centropomus viridis)				
Sorubim (Pseudoplatystoma spp.)				
Spearfish				
Atlantic (Tetrapturus spp.)				
Shortbill (Tetrapturus angustirostris)				
Splake (Salvelinus fontinalis x namaycush)				
Spotted Seatrout (Cynoscion nebulosus)				
Sturgeon (Acipenseridae spp.)				
Sunfish				
Green (Lepomis cyanellus)				
Redbreast (Lepomis auritus)				
Redear (Lepomis microlophus)				
Swordfish (Xiphias gladius)				
Taimen (Hucho taimen)				
Tambaqui (Colossoma macropomum)				
Tarpon (Megalops spp.)				
Tautog (Tautoga onitis)				
Tench (Tinca tinca)				
Threadfin				
Giant African (Polydactylus quadrifilis)				
King (Polydactylus macrochir)				
Tigerfish (Hydrocynus vittatus)				
Tigerfish, Goliath (Hydrocynus goliath)				
Trahira (Hoplias malabaricus)				
Trevally				
Bigeye (Caranx sexfasciatus)				
Bluefin (Caranx melampygus)				
Giant (Caranx ignobilis)				

Fishing Life List

Species	Date	Lure/Bait	Specs	Location
Golden (*Gnathanodon speciosus*)				
Tripletail (*Lobotes surinamensis*)				
Trout				
Brook (*Salvelinus fontinalis*)				
Brown (*Salmo trutta*)				
Bull (*Salvelinus confluentus*)				
Cutthroat (*Oncorhynchus clarkia*)				
Dolly Varden (*Salvenlinus malma*)				
Golden (*Oncorhynchus aguabonita*)				
Lake (*Salvelinus namaycush*)				
Rainbow (*Oncorhynchus mykiss*)				
Tiger (*Salmo trutta × Salvelinus fontinalis*)				
Tuna				
Bigeye (*Thunnus obesus*)				
Blackfin (*Thunnus atlanticus*)				
Bluefin (*Thunnus thynnus*)				
Dogtooth (*Gymnosarda unicolor*)				
Longtail (*Thunnus tonggol*)				
Pacific Bluefin (*Thunnus orientalis*)				
Skipjack (*Katsuwonus pelamis*)				
Southern Bluefin (*Thunnus maccoyii*)				
Yellowfin (*Thunnus albacares*)				
Wahoo (*Acanthocybium solandri*)				
Walleye (*Sander vitreus*)				
Warmouth (*Lepomis gulosus*)				
Weakfish (*Cynoscion regalis*)				
Wels Catfish (*Silurus glanis*)				
Whitefish				
Lake (*Coregonus clupeaformis*)				
Mountain (*Prosopium williamsoni*)				
Round (*Prosopium cylindraceum*)				
Zander (*Sander lucioperca*)				

Species	Date	Lure/Bait	Specs	Location

Fishing Life List

Species	Date	Lure/Bait	Specs	Location

Species	Date	Lure/Bait	Specs	Location

Fishing Life List

Species	Date	Lure/Bait	Specs	Location

Species	Date	Lure/Bait	Specs	Location

Fishing Life List

Species	Date	Lure/Bait	Specs	Location

Species	Date	Lure/Bait	Specs	Location

Fishing Life List

Species	Date	Lure/Bait	Specs	Location

Species	Date	Lure/Bait	Specs	Location

Fishing Life List

Species	Date	Lure/Bait	Specs	Location

Species	Date	Lure/Bait	Specs	Location

Photo Gallery
Add your best fishing photographs to make an epic angling scrapbook!

About the Artist

Nick Mayer is an award-winning nature illustrator whose style embraces the natural beauty of fish and other marine life with a unique scientific perspective. He is a former marine biologist, an adventurer, and a lifelong fly-fishing addict. A survival after falling overboard off a commercial fishing vessel into the Bering Sea, followed by a float plane near-crash in Northern Labrador, inspired Nick to pursue his true calling as an artist.

www.nickmayerart.com

All images by Nick Mayer unless noted below.

Shutterstock: page 1 hook vector 3D Vector; pages 6 and 7 icons Dmitry Rubanik; pages 8 and 9 icons Vakabungo; pages 10 and 11 icons SkyPics Studio; page 146 frame Robyn Mackenzie; pages 146–159 background wash Ratana21

ISBN 978-1-64178-080-3

Fox Chapel Publishing makes every effort to use environmentally friendly paper for printing.

We are always looking for talented authors and artists. To submit an idea, please send a brief inquiry to acquisitions@foxchapelpublishing.com.

Printed in Singapore
First printing